Ready To Craft Your Course?

Cover art and illustrations by Ferdinando Rihi & Gabriel Yoofi

Editor: Amy du Toit

Book Production and Publishing Services by Miramare Ponte Press, LLC
www.miramarepontepress.com

Hardback ISBN-13: 979-8-9875530-7-7
Paperback ISBN-13: 979-8-9875530-6-0
eBook ISBN-13: 979-8-9875530-5-3

Kankam-Boateng, Charles
Parallel Lanes/Charles Kankam-Boateng
*Contact info@lionsmatrix.com or visit www.lionsmatrix.com to bulk purchase Parallel Lanes: Choose Your Destiny Now!

A receipt will be issued for tax purposes.
hc: 979-8-9875530-7-7

DEDICATION

To Dad and Mom, the epitome of Putting Education First

To my wife, Theresa,
and children, Lionel, Lillian and Legend

My Joy!

HOLD OUT YOUR HANDS. DO YOU SEE HOW EACH OF YOUR FINGERS POINT FORWARD CREATING THEIR OWN INDIVIDUAL LANE?

AS YOU CONTINUE TO GROW, YOU'LL FIND LIFE LOOKS JUST LIKE THIS. MANY PATHS TO CHOOSE FROM, EACH OFFERING A HIT OR A MISS.

WORKING OUT WHICH ROUTES TO TAKE CAN BE CONFUSING, BUT IF WE STAY DETERMINED AND RESILIENT, LISTEN TO THE WISDOM OF THOSE WHO HAVE TRAVELLED BEFORE US, AND MAKE GOOD CHOICES, WE CAN ACHIEVE OUR DREAMS.

BEFORE WE START, IT'S IMPORTANT YOU REMEMBER THAT JUST LIKE NATURE MOVES THROUGH DIFFERENT SEASONS, SO DO OUR LIVES.

SOMETIMES WE ARE IN **SPRING**, WHERE OUR LIFE IS BURSTING WITH NEW BEGINNINGS AND POSITIVE GROWTH AS WE EMBRACE CHANGE.

Welcome to High School

THEN COMES **FALL**, THESE ARE SEASONS OF TRANSITION. JUST LIKE LEAVES CHANGE COLOR AND BEGIN TO DROP, SOMETIMES WE NEED TO LET GO OF THINGS WE ENJOY SO WE CAN MOVE ONTO SOMETHING EVEN BETTER.

UNIVERSITY

Other times can feel just like **summer**. The world around us is vibrant, days are full and fun, we flourish, work hard, and reap the rewards of our efforts.

Winter seasons feel hard... aggh. Like in nature where trees are bare, the ground is slippery and animals go into hiding, life's winter seasons force us to stop. We might lose something we love or feel a little lonely and lost, but if we use the time to think and resync, we'll soon be back on track.

Each season is equally important and all have a purpose in helping us grow, so don't try to run but embrace each one.

LIKE IT OR NOT, EDUCATION IS THE KEY WHICH UNLOCKS YOUR FUTURE.
"A READER TODAY, A LEADER TOMORROW!"
SO, DIVE INTO YOUR STUDIES, FIND A WAY TO LEARN THAT SUITS YOUR
SPECIFIC STYLE, AND BE SURE TO FEED YOUR MIND JUST LIKE YOU
FEED YOUR BODY.
THE LIFE YOU ARRIVE AT AS AN ADULT WILL BE DIRECTLY IMPACTED BY
WHAT YOU DO NOW.

BY HOW YOU THINK ABOUT YOURSELF
AND THE WORLD AROUND YOU.

BY THE QUESTIONS YOU ARE BRAVE ENOUGH
TO ASK (DON'T BE AFRAID TO CHALLENGE
THINGS THAT DON'T SEEM RIGHT TO YOU)!

By the relationships you keep and the networks you grow.

And by your personal commitment to growth and excellence.

Will you choose the education lane kiddo?

Yessss!

DID YOU KNOW OUR MINDS ARE LIKE ELASTIC, MEANING WE CAN STRETCH AND EXPAND THEM!

INTELLIGENCE ISN'T SOMETHING WE ARE BORN WITH, IT'S DEVELOPED OVER TIME WHEN WE CHOOSE TO LIVE A LIFE OF CONTINUAL LEARNING. BUT NOT EVERYONE CHOOSES THIS LANE.

CRITICISMS

COMPARISON

INSECURITIES

DEFENSIVENESS

INHIBITED GROWTH

SOME PEOPLE HAVE WHAT'S CALLED A FIXED MINDSET. THEY DON'T ENJOY CHALLENGES. THEY BELIEVE THEY CAN EITHER DO SOMETHING NATURALLY, OR THEY CAN'T, AND WHEN THEY FAIL, THEY STOP.

FIXED MINDSET

"I STICK TO WHAT I KNOW AND WHEN I'M FRUSTRATED, I GIVE UP!"

#3: ENVY ALLEY

"BLESSED IS HE WHO HAS LEARNED TO ADMIRE BUT NOT ENVY, TO FOLLOW BUT NOT IMITATE, TO PRAISE BUT NOT FLATTER, AND TO LEAD BUT NOT MANIPULATE" WILLIAM ARTHUR WARD.

ENVY ALLEY IS A PERILOUS PATH. WHEN YOU TURN GREEN WITH ENVY AT THE SUCCESS OR WEALTH OF ANOTHER, RATHER THAN CELEBRATING ALONGSIDE THEM, YOU ARE OPENING YOURSELF UP TO THE DARK FUSION OF JEALOUSY, BITTERNESS, AND LONELINESS.

REFUSING TO HIT 'LIKE', PUSHING OUT HOSTILE COMMENTS AND TRYING TO BE BETTER THAN OTHERS MIGHT FEEL LIKE A NATURAL RESPONSE, YET IT ONLY LEADS TO YOUR OWN DOWNFALL AS YOUR INFLUENCE AND IDENTITY DISAPPEARS. CHOOSE TO BE DIFFERENT. BE RESPECTFUL AND IF SOMEONE HAS A NEGATIVE IMPACT ON YOU, UNFOLLOW THEM.

HAPPINESS MAY COME AND GO REAL FAST, BUT JOY IS FOREVER, IT WILL ALWAYS LAST.

A CHANGE OF CIRCUMSTANCE, AN ARGUMENT, A LOSS OR FAILURE CAN SOON STEAL HAPPINESS AWAY, BUT JOY... IT IS A DEEP INNER DELIGHT THAT CANNOT EASILY BE SHAKEN.

THINK OF IT LIKE THIS: WHILE HAPPINESS IS A POPSICLE ON A HOT SUMMER'S DAY THAT SOON MELTS, JOY IS THE CARNIVAL MEMORIES THAT LAST A LIFETIME.

THOSE WHO CHOOSE THE JOY LANE ARE INTENTIONAL AND GRATEFUL. THEY APPRECIATE WHAT THEY HAVE (EVEN IF IT'S NOT AS GRAND AS EVERYONE ELSE'S) AND UNDERSTAND THAT LIFE ITSELF IS THE ULTIMATE GIFT.

#5: Mind Your Own Business Boulevard

Have you noticed how busy some people are meddling and peddling in the affairs of others?! They spend so much time looking at what everyone else is doing they forget they have their own race to run.

Why insert yourself into someone else's drama, when you can create your own story by:

1. Respecting the privacy and boundaries of others.

2. Choosing not to listen to, comment on or share the personal information of others.

We all have to make decisions in life. Some are easy and come naturally, while others are BIG and have significant consequences. When evaluating our choices, it's important to learn from our own experiences and the wisdom of people we trust, like our elders and mentors.

Remember, you are in control of your own life story. Don't try to please others, or choose lanes just because those around you are. Take charge and make decisions that are true to yourself. Just like Jeff Bezos, who had a regular job but followed his dreams to create Amazon. Even when people doubted him, he knew he had to take a chance and go down an unknown path.

While it's good to listen to advice from your parents, teachers, and friends, don't be afraid to think for yourself. Take their guidance into consideration, but in the end, it's up to you to decide what's best for you.

Friend, one right decision can be life-changing, and so can one wrong one. Know your options, be an independent thinker, find your own purpose, and be brave in crafting your own course. There's a superhero in you, I know it!

Author's Biography

Charles, the CEO of LionsMatrix: The Ultimate Growth Matrix, is dedicated to inspiring growth in both kids and adults. With over a decade of IT experience, he's consulted for Fortune 500 companies, embracing diverse leadership styles. Charles is also a charismatic speaker and an MBA graduate.

Passionate about enriching young minds, he loves speaking at schools, libraries, and events. Beyond his professional endeavors, Charles is known as The Meaning Maker—a storyteller who helps us find significance in our lives and experiences. When not immersed in his professional work, he enjoys reading, listening to podcasts, hiking, sightseeing, and traveling. He resides in Atlanta, Georgia, with his wife and children. He continually strives to lift lives and build potential through his work.

If you like to stay inspired or connect, check out his website www.lionsmatrix.com

Parallel Lanes - Choose Your Destiny Now!

LIONSMATRIX
THE ULTIMATE GROWTH MATRIX